Managing
Brainpower

Managing Brainpower
includes three volumes:
Book One: Organizing
Book Two: Measuring
Book Three: Selling

Chuck Thomsen

Managing Brainpower

Organizing, Measuring Performance, and Selling in Architecture, Engineering, and Construction Management Companies

Book Two: Measuring

The American Institute of Architects Press
Washington, D.C.

The American Institute of Architects Press
1735 New York Avenue, N.W.
Washington, D.C. 20006

Library of Congress Cataloging-in-Publication Data
Thomsen, Chuck.
Managing brainpower.

   Contents: v. 1. Organizing—v. 2. Measuring—v. 3. Selling.
   1. Architectural practice—Management. 2. Architectural services
marketing. 3. Engineering—Management. 4. Engineering services
marketing. 5. Construction industry—Management. 6. Construction
industry—Marketing. I. Title.
NA1996.T47 1989   720'.68   89-17620
ISBN 1-55835-001-2 (set)

Designed by Robert Hickey, Arlington, Virginia
Printed by McNaughton & Gunn, Saline, Michigan

To
A. C. "Deac" Esterly, AIA,
of Springfield, Missouri,
my mentor and good friend, who cared for his
clients as much as any architect I know.

CONTENTS

Introduction

Financial reports are generally accepted as necessary for tax planning, banking relations, and determining the price of services, but they are also the means to reward people fairly, motivate behavior, facilitate delegation, and provide feedback for control. They are the company scoreboard.

A lot of good professionals denigrate accounting. They assume that if they do their work well and serve their clients well, the bottom line will take care of itself. They're seldom right. Many firms lose money when they're busiest; projects can be so demanding that no one takes the time to manage. Without day-to-day control over money and man-hours, a firm's profitability can vanish.

No firm can do good work for long without genuine profits. Knee-jerk cost cutting turns off the turned-on people. Everyone loses confidence—in themselves and in management. Morale deteriorates. Managers who don't measure the ebb and flow of money and man-hours inevitably treat their employees inequitably—for two reasons. First, they may not really be sure who is earning for the company. Second, they won't have the money to reward the high performers.

Why have a scoreboard? Most professionals recognize that they should know how much money they make. They accept conventional reasons for producing financial reports: They don't want to run afoul of the Internal Revenue Service; they must supply financial information if they need occasional help from a bank; they must know what it costs to do business to quote proper fees for future projects.

If financial reports are properly structured, they provide four other benefits. First, they help determine who is performing and should be rewarded. Second, they motivate. Third, they facilitate delegation and autonomy. Fourth, they provide the feedback essential for control.

Financial reports allow you to reward people fairly. In a manufacturing company, money is invested in materials and technology to produce future cash flows. In a professional service company, money is invested in people. Money is a carrot, used to attract and keep good brains. It is vital to measure the return on investment in people so they can be fairly rewarded.

Measurement affects behavior. Students study harder the night before an exam. Measurement and scoring motivate people and also focus attention on the important issues. Consider a basketball game. Without a scoreboard, players would probably show off with fancy dribbles and hotdog stunts. Teamwork would suffer. But if there is a scoreboard, everybody's attention is focused on the major purpose of the organization—sinking baskets *and winning!*

You can hurt the company by measuring only part of its activity. If the sole measure of performance is financial, service and innovation will suffer.

And even within the financial area, concentration on only part of the results can cause problems. We once decided that projects were the heart of the company's profitability. According to our thinking, if the projects were profitable, the rest of the company would be fine. We focused on project profitability to the exclusion of other measures of expense. We jumped on managers when their multiples fell. The project multiple was the brightest light on the scoreboard.

So what happened? We certainly affected behavior. We motivated our employees to charge their time and expenses to overhead accounts whenever possible. We motivated our salaried employees not to record overtime. Our reports showed that our projects cost less than they really did, our overhead was high, and the habit of not charging time to projects shortchanged us on cost-plus contracts.

Many years ago, I had a light-hearted, freewheeling conversation with a group of colleagues at Rice University about the office of the future. One fellow suggested that we put various benign radioactive substances in pencil lead and then measure the radioactivity of each substance in a set of tracings to determine who put the most lead on paper. Another predicted that drafting rooms would be set up with closed-circuit TV cameras. The boss could check up on what everyone was doing just by switching from one camera to another. We had the usual view of the future: technology as a tool of oppression—"Big Brother Is Watching You."

Well, we didn't monitor people with TV cameras or radioactive substances. We did it with computers. And it wasn't oppressive. It created freedom for middle management, supported entrepreneurship, and flattened the pyramid.

Before computers and management information systems, people had to watch people to know what was going on. Managers felt they knew how the work should be done and how to make money. They gave firm direction so that things would be done the way they wanted. And they watched those who reported to them to make sure they did what they were told.

Computers and management information systems make it easier to delegate responsibility and accountability. Leaders know what other people are doing because they have reports on their performance. Because these performance reports can be quickly produced and understood, leaders can increase the number of people reporting to them and thereby delegate more authority.

Finally, financial reports help by providing feedback for control. Think of money as an analogue of effort. Then think of financial reports as windows into the company. Our clients ask us to work for them, and they pay us for that work. We do the same with our employees. If financial reports are formatted to match the organization, they can tell you what people are doing and how project teams are performing.

No control system will work without feedback. If you drive a car, you constantly look around and ahead and make small adjustments to the controls. You are continually making on-course corrections. Your eyes are the feedback system. To control money and man-hours properly, you must also measure where you are and look ahead. Financial reports are part of the feedback system.

A principle of control systems is that drift is a function of feedback *frequency*. What that means isn't hard to grasp. The more frequently you look at the road, the more gentle the steering corrections will be. But if you turn to talk to a passenger, you may have to swerve violently to keep from drifting into a fire plug.

The same applies to management. As with all other systems, the frequency of feedback will affect the degree of severity of the company's management reactions.

CHAPTER 1

Rewards

Increasing pay won't increase productivity, but fairness and the promise of income growth are necessary to keep good people. Growth companies expect hard work and deliver rewards for good performance.

COMPENSATION

Like other management concepts, ideas about compensation are influenced by industrial traditions. Many of these ideas assume that people don't like to work. They assume that people work for pay, not pleasure. So industrial managers use money to attract labor. With the compelling help of unions and personnel departments, they devise benefits and fringes and rely on newsletters or outside activities such as baseball teams to create company spirit.

Brainpower companies are different. For the best people—the ones they most want—the primary attraction is intellectual, not financial. More pay won't improve the quality of work or increase productivity. Big salaries alone will neither attract nor keep the best people.

That doesn't mean that you don't have to pay good people what they are worth. Good people who feel underpaid will leave, and competitive, entrepreneurial people will work hard for a bonus. But it may be the competition and the scorecard as much as the compensation that produce results.

Maximizing income growth

Productivity is not a function of pay. It is a function of productive people. But productive people are attracted and stimulated by income growth. They want to grow economically as well as professionally. As long as they progress and know that future rewards are there, they will strive for success. The rate of increase in compensation has more effect than the absolute amount. Promotions and raises make people feel wonderful.

Good firms can do four simple things to provide income growth and the stimulating vision of future rewards:

1. Hire graduates directly from school. Recruit the best of the class. If you compromise your selection, you compromise your future. Find ambitious people who are looking for postgraduate training and offer them a chance to work with brilliant people.

You must be good enough to attract the best for no more than the market rate. You don't want those whose only interest is short-term pay.

2. Expect hard work. Few professionals succeed on forty hours a week. Fire the nine-to-fivers; they'll mess up the system. Good people are driven by pride and ambition; they work hard because hard work is part of the culture and because their leaders set a fierce pace.

3. Deliver the rewards. If your firm does good work, you'll grow. If you grow, you can promote people rapidly. And when you promote people, you can increase their pay more than the rate of inflation. When your people deliver, you must deliver, too. Provide a fast track for high performers and keep the deadwood out.

There must be significant rewards at the higher rungs. In great companies, youngsters work for experience, education, and the chance to be around high performers. Senior management makes a bundle. In mediocre companies, entry jobs get top dollar while inept leaders eke out a living.

As people reach the top of a company, salary increases level off, and compensation comes more from bonuses and ownership. Individual success becomes more tied to the success of the company.

4. Customize compensation to responsibility. The basis for compensation is as important as the amount of compensation. And the structure of compensation should fit the job.

There are many ways to pay people. You can give them a guaranteed salary, a part of profits, ownership, and perks. Group leaders who make profit and loss decisions and run a tight ship should share in their profits. They may also be rewarded with stock for helping the company. People who are directed in their work by a manager should receive a fair salary whether the company succeeds or not.

WHO SETS PAY?

Compensation decisions should be delegated along the organizational lines of the firm to people who know the performers and are qualified to evaluate their work. Committees can advise and help achieve parity, but ultimate authority must rest with group leaders.

The most common reason companies don't grow is that leadership won't delegate. Nowhere is that more true than in managing compensation.

The people who evaluate individual performance should make compensation decisions. There are enormous differences in productivity between one person and the next, but you can't tell that simply by looking at the people, by measuring their experience, or by checking their degrees or job descriptions. To pay people fairly, you must know them and know the results they produce. That means authority to set compensation must be pushed down in the organization.

Setting salaries and bonuses for individuals is the work of individuals. The more people involved in deciding on an individual's salary, the more the salary is apt to be increased. Another downfall of a committee is the tendency to produce average raises that cheat stars and reward mediocrity.

The delegation of salary decisions must follow the basic lines of the organization. No one wants to work for someone who has no say in his or her pay. And managers who have the responsibility for the top and bottom lines of the company must also have the authority to decide how to spend the part in between.

Decentralized compensation management solves these problems. It also causes some. Within a single company, group managers should approach compensation with similar attitudes, but there will always be inconsistencies. Since people transfer from one group to another, one group leader will inherit another's compensation decisions. Some will be too generous, others too stingy. You need equality. You want group leaders to control salaries (and you want the people working for them to know it), but you don't want ten different salary programs in the same company.

3D/International formed a compensation committee of peers that set guidelines, advised, and reviewed raises proposed by group leaders. Final authority rested with the group leaders. But group leaders take advice from the committee because they respect the good people we put on it.

What do you do if a group manager disagrees with the committee? Let the manager decide— unless there are too many bad calls. Then find a new manager.

PERFORMANCE REVIEWS

The market controls salaries. Performance ranks people within the market, but finally salary is a function of supply and demand.

In one of his monologues, Bill Cosby claims that he and his wife are intellectuals. Before their first child, they studied natural childbirth. He then delivers the punch line, which goes something like this: "*Intellectuals are people who study how to do things that other people do naturally.*"

Well, to paraphrase Cosby, managers tend to bureaucratize what should be done naturally. Nowhere is that more true than in the performance review process. And few acts of management can be more destructive.

Performance and the market

Most managers tell employees that performance governs compensation. That's not quite true. The market controls compensation; performance positions people within the marketplace.

Professional service firms compete in two markets simultaneously: They sell labor to clients, and they buy labor from the work force. Each transaction must be done competitively. The market for each controls the raises. It's misleading to tell employees that performance alone determines their pay.

Yes, performance affects pay. You can pay more for productive people. Supply and demand set the price, and good performance is always in short supply. Performance also affects job security and results in promotions to higher rungs on the ladder.

But eventually, the market dominates compensation. If the market for people goes up, you must meet it. If it goes down, you must restrain raises, decrease salaries, or replace some high-paid people in order to stay competitive. If you hire people for too much, you must hold down their raises even if performance is good.

So it's a mistake to link employee reviews directly to salary reviews. If you do, sooner or later you may have to explain a paltry raise after a superior performance review. Then both the salary review and performance review will lose credibility.

Here's an example of what I mean: In the eighties the Texas building economy went into a slump. Building permits in Houston fell from $260 million per month to $60 million per month. Architects and engineers were on the street or driving cabs. Although 3D/I's practice was national and international, we were severely affected. We had to tell those great people who were working doubly hard to keep us afloat that we couldn't increase their salaries. It wasn't fair, but it was necessary.

Many managers feel that if people work hard and do good work they should get a raise, no matter how much they make to start with. Eventually these companies will be populated by a lot of overpaid senior people whose productivity is decreasing. No one will have the heart to decrease their salaries.

Employee evaluation forms

Most personnel evaluation forms are worthless. They address mundane issues. They use criteria such as "responds to directions cheerfully," "dresses well," and "does neat work" but never cover such relevant points as "tells the boss when the boss is wrong," "listens and responds to clients," "leads criticism of poor corporate procedures." Few forms ask employees to say what their bosses should do to help them function more effectively.

Some forms even have boxes for scores. Reviewers calculate grades based on subjective assumptions associated with incomplete and arbitrary lists of "universally desirable employee qualities." Then they flash a self-satisfied smile and say, "*Look! We have an objective evaluation system.*"

A few actually suggest that these scores should be used to determine raises. That's pseudologic: The precision of the process exceeds the accuracy of the assumptions.

Here is an example of the flaws in this process. Most criteria sets I've seen include the question, "Does he/she dress well?" How do you judge? Maybe you establish such objective corporate standards as:

6. buys at Brooks Brothers

5. attire is a little trendy

4. wears tweeds and elbow patches

3. wears double-knit polyester

2. works in jeans and running shoes

1. wears running shorts to work

What do you do with that score? Say you are reviewing a supertalented, hard-working engineer. He wears jeans and running shoes at the office. His pay is 25 percent below the market, he is being courted by competitors, and you need people. If you're smart, you'll junk the score, give him a big raise, and ask him politely to spruce up a little if he doesn't mind. Say *"Please."*

Here are the problems you face in using review forms:

Question sets produce averages. Forms level people with great talent and glaring weaknesses to mundane mediocrity. Mozart would have received a ten for "understands job well" but a zero for "works well with fellow employees." The averaged result: an average score for a pretty nonaverage fellow. Most exceptional people I've known have exceptional flaws as well. You can't compute averages in evaluating talent.

The written review is annual, but the underground review is daily. We all get feedback every time we do something—good or bad. These daily reviews, not the annual ones, shape performance.

"Good" and "great" are the standard in written reviews. Look at the personnel files of fired employees and you'll seldom find a bad review. Written reviews rarely reflect real opinions.

No question set is ever appropriate. People have an infinite variety of strengths and weaknesses. No one can ever create the universal form to cover them all. I've known people who have lost their jobs because of unattractive attributes that had nothing to do with performance.

3D/I's chief legal counsel and administrative officer, Jerry Hoover, isn't as flip as I about these evaluations. He points out that in these litigious days of EEO suits, a firm had better have documentation when it fires someone. Sad but true. The only real use for personnel evaluation forms is to protect the company, not to help employees.

The review process

Although performance review forms are ineffective, I believe in talking with employees on a regular basis to discuss their contributions to the company—and vice versa. Here are my thoughts on how to do it:

Make evaluations goal oriented. You have to know what employees want to achieve before you can help them. If you can relate their goals to company goals, you help both the employee and the company.

Institutionalize schedules. If you don't have a formal schedule for evaluations, some people will never get around to doing them. Evaluations should occur more than once a year. Lee Iacocca believes in quarterly goal reviews. Kenneth Blanchard and Spencer Johnson, authors of *The One Minute Manager*, preach constant feedback.

Establish priorities. When you evaluate employees, you need to distinguish major problems from minor irritations and separate long-range career ambitions from passing interests. Keep the long-range view uppermost, for the firm's sake as well as for the employee's.

Watch your biases. First impressions are generally formed from the characteristics that commonly appear on review forms: dress, style, personality, diligence. First impressions tend to be biased, though; they should give way to a balanced assessment of hard results once you've had an opportunity to evaluate an employee's work and his or her ability to build teams and work with clients.

Both methods of judging can be misleading. But the most misleading of all is that charming, respectful, attractive person who strokes your ego and does mediocre work.

Make reviews two-way. It's revealing to learn how your employees think of your job. Ask people what you can do to help them—and vice versa. You may discover that you need to clarify your job. You may also get some good advice.

Rank employees. Get your key leaders together and rank your employees—first draft choice, second choice. Don't worry about specific criteria. Just decide who is most valuable to you, who is next, and so on down the line. Then if you have to fire someone, fire from the bottom.

Be sure, though, that those doing the ranking *know* the people being ranked. I've seen promising careers interrupted by managers who either didn't know what was going on or sometimes allowed personality conflicts to trigger unfair judgments.

SALARIES

Salaries are the most basic form of compensation; yet no other area of management deals with more complexities. Across-the-board equity at any given moment is impossible to achieve.

In a brainpower company, the subjective factors that complicate the whole process make salary management well nigh unmanageable. Here are some of the problems:

The wonderful human virtues of friendship, compassion, and generosity become vices when you're making compensation decisions. Then, being tough-minded becomes a virtue.

Most people overestimate their importance to the company. A few underestimate. Almost no one sees it as it actually is, and if everyone were equitably paid, few would see it that way.

There is no infallible system that measures the productivity of brainpower. Managers who know what people are doing and who are *qualified to evaluate* must make judgments. That means compensation decisions are decentralized, and decentralized policies are inevitably applied unevenly.

There is confusion between paying the person and the position. Should an individual receive an annual salary of $75,000 because he or she is a project manager? Or should a project manager be paid more or less depending on who the individual is?

When by mistake, or as an expediency during growth, you hire people for a premium, the rest of your employees will judge the higher salaries proper and grow discontented with their own.

Some companies pay more than others. If you pay the market average, your people will learn about a company that pays more and feel slighted.

Some people are paid premiums to switch companies. They disclose their new salaries to their old colleagues. Everyone views the premium as the market standard.

So you have problems. You always will; inequities are inevitable. Why? Because you can rarely decrease salaries. A ratchet is built into compensation, and it's locked in the up position. But raising everyone's salary to compensate for each individual disparity will ratchet you out of business.

Here are some attitudes and ideas that help in managing salaries:

Maintain flexibility. You can't solve the perplexing problems of compensation with rules. Rigid compensation policies are designed by managers who are reluctant or unable to make decisions about people as individuals or who lack confidence. They need rules to hide behind. Rules can't eliminate the problems of discontent and inequity.

People are individual and policies are categorical. When we treat people categorically, we sidestep our obligation to judge the individual. Perhaps fixed job descriptions and the need to deal with large groups of people require fixed pay levels in industrial companies, but in professional service companies we buy brainpower. The ever-present danger is in abdicating our responsibility to deal with individuals individually.

Although policies should be flexible, salary reviews should be discussed formally—not instigated by an employee on an airplane or in a restaurant.

Review individuals, but review them in groups. If you give people raises one at a time, you won't be consistent, and the total amount of increases will probably be higher than if you review people in groups. Looking at people comparatively increases objectivity and minimizes impulsive rewards. You are more inclined to make choices, to differentiate. But whatever you do, don't give blanket raises; they're demeaning.

Review salaries annually. Although performance reviews should be conducted more often, salary reviews should be based on a full year's performance. And it's important to make sure that annual review dates are honored; people get upset, and justifiably so, when those dates are allowed to slip.

Avoid ad hoc raises in general—but consider exceptions. One exception is the valuable employee who is honestly underpaid, thus leaving the firm vulnerable to a successful pick-off attempt by a competitor; rectify those situations immediately. Another is the employee who has earned a battle-field promotion; the raise that should accompany that promotion will be a vote of confidence, and it's usually worth more than the risk taken in violating the ad-hoc raise prohibition. Just don't make the raise too big; leave something in reserve for the annual review.

Be reluctant to make an exception for the employee who threatens to quit for a better paying job. Don't get into a bidding war; it tells other employees that they, too, can get raises if they can find better offers elsewhere.

Knee-jerk raises are a mistake, but it's fatal not to reward performers over the long haul. Employees must feel confident that you will treat them fairly. The only way to develop that confidence is to deliver.

Pay market value. I've never hired anyone for more than he or she has asked for—but I've given quick raises to many people who were worth more than their entry salaries. It's tempting to take advantage of people who'll work for less than they're worth, but it's bad business; you soon lose them to firms willing to pay them fairly. Turnover is expensive, and it interrupts projects.

Don't overpay, either. A good company doesn't pay premiums. Salary potential is a strong motivation, but it is the opportunity for responsibility and recognition that attracts the kind of people you want.

I've heard people rationalize paying a high salary for someone in a cost-reimbursable position. That's a grave error. Their salary will leak out, causing other employees—and maybe your client—to feel mistreated. And at the end of the job, you'll have an overpaid employee whose salary has set a new implied pay standard in the organization.

Have a wide range of raises. In determining a raise, consider the percentage of increase but also consider a person's *absolute* worth to the company. People who show no increase in productivity merit no increase. (You should probably replace them.) People who maintain the same level of responsibility but improve performance deserve adequate raises. And truly exceptional performers deserve exceptional raises.

Promote from within. Hiring experienced people makes your job easier, but it minimizes opportunities for promotions and raises. Hire young people with less experience and more potential. If you hire young people at lower salaries than your average, you will dilute the average salary and allow substantial raises for good performers. And as the young people advance, their increased responsibilities quickly earn them more money. That's a win-win situation.

Avoid compassion. It is unfair to reward someone who needs it instead of someone else who has earned it.

Change the rules for international compensation. For employees in the U.S., you don't have to consider individual needs. Assuming comparable performance, you pay the same salary to a single person as to one with a spouse and six children.

When you send project people overseas, you buy new headaches: You become involved in your employee's family life. You provide housing, education for school-age children. And to convince the best people to go, you may have to design individual packages.

International compensation has to be adapted for the country and the times. In the days of the Saudi Arabian boom, we attached all kinds of bells and whistles to foreign salary. We'd start with a base salary, add a foreign service premium and a completion bonus, pay for housing, cars, home leave, compassion leave, foreign education for children, and reimbursement for the additional income taxes charged on all those perks. A base salary of $50,000 could grow quickly to $150,000.

The Saudi work supported these fringe benefits and demanded them. Despite the wonderful professional challenge, Saudi Arabia lacked many of the amenities of home. And because the economy back home was good, we had to pay premiums to get people to go.

But then we and other American companies applied the same perks to the Far East. Our Malaysian office failed because of it. Our Hong Kong office almost failed before we realized that in order to be competitive, we had to treat every employee as a local. That meant we had to hire only those people who *wanted* to work overseas—at locally competitive rates.

Overtime

Labor laws require overtime pay for clerks, not for professionals. Yet many firms pay overtime for young professionals. This practice ultimately hurts the quality of work and the culture of the company.

When you pay overtime to professionals, you're forced to limit it, or your costs will run out of control. And limiting it means telling your employees that they can't put out extra effort. They can't work all night to do a great job. Or you will have to tell them that it's okay to do more work, but they can't record it on their time sheets. That messes up your records and sounds shady to your employees.

In a brainpower company, top management always works unusual hours. Barring young professionals from overtime work eliminates the wonderfully educational experience of putting in extra effort alongside the firm's top people.

Furthermore, one of our most common problems is resource leveling. Our clients don't want to arrange their needs for our convenience. So sometimes we have all-night work sessions; then everyone sleeps in the next morning. Intellectual energy doesn't come from people in convenient nine-to-five brackets, and neither does the demand for it.

Successful people work endlessly. The habit should start when they join the company. Great work often comes from ordinary people who deliver extraordinary effort. Great companies are populated by tireless people.

Hard work produces quality, quality produces growth, and growth provides opportunity. A no-growth firm must fire, retire, or bury people to provide promotions. Growth companies can provide far more opportunities. You can't promise people that if they work hard the company will grow. But you can point out that the chances are better if they do.

PERKS

Perks are important carrots, but when they're too far out of reach they generate resentment instead of incentive.

One attitude toward business reflects the idea that a company's purpose is to serve its owners: The company is a conduit for wealth and status for the people who own it. Owners take all the perks they can as tax-free income. That theory works fine when ownership is closely held and capital or long-term growth are not goals.

But as more people share ownership, funds must be used more objectively to be fair to all shareholders. The company is viewed as the mother lode rather than as a conduit. It becomes a growing asset. Owners realize that it's shortsighted to weaken the company for short-term personal gain, when long-term gains may be greater.

Tax-motivated company perks deserve scrutiny

I've seen people get so paranoid about taxes that they do all kinds of expensive things to avoid them. Company-paid perks are an excellent example; they create cost. Employees who buy their own cars won't spend as much as they will if the company pays for them. Restaurants that cater to expense accounts cost more than family restaurants. Most corporate executives spend more on their office furniture than on their home furniture. Somehow people have come to believe that extravagance is okay if it's tax deductible. A lot of cost is created in the name of tax avoidance.

Self-image and personal values play a major role where perks are involved. I have known good leaders who find flying coach a little demeaning. Others feel it's wasteful to fly first class. One believes that the company benefits from increased productivity during and after a first-class flight; the other talks about fiscal prudence.

An enormous gap in status exists between labor and management in industry. In capital-intensive companies, the owners too often don't treat hired employees equally. But in a company that sells brainpower, too much disparity develops a destructive "we-they" attitude.

If the leaders of a brainpower company are extravagant, their employees will follow their lead. It takes restraint to set an example. When you control the purse strings, you can easily convince yourself that you deserve more.

BONUSES

Bonuses are valid as a profit incentive. They won't work as a salary supplement, and as an act of generosity they are destructive.

Here's an interesting test. Ask people who received bonuses why they got them. If your experience is like mine, you'll get confused answers. Some people will tell you that their management is generous when times are good. Others will say that bonuses are a reward for hard work. Others will explain that they are a standard part of compensation. Then ask managers why they pay bonuses. I'll give you odds you will get a different set of answers altogether.

Most people don't understand the purpose of an incentive bonus program. And if they don't know what it's for, there's no incentive. You're wasting your money.

What should a bonus be?

A reward for hard work? When you hire someone you should look that person square in the eye and say: "*Here is our deal. For the salary that you and I agree on, we want all your professional dedication. We aren't renting your intellectual vigor for eight hours a day; we want it all.*"

You should expect dedication and hard work. The reward for exceptional performance should be exceptional pay plus fast promotion—not a bonus.

Generosity? Bonuses aren't gifts, and you shouldn't expect employees to feel grateful for them. Compensation is not an act of good will. People should realize that they earn their pay. It improves self-esteem. It establishes a healthy cause-and-effect relationship between good pay and good profits.

Don't tell people their bonuses are the result of executive generosity. Tell them the truth: They came from profits they made.

Salary supplement? The first architect I worked for was Deac Esterly in Springfield, Missouri. He was typical of many of the solid professionals who operate in smaller cities in America. He paid me a salary that covered rent and groceries. If he made money, he added a bonus. That made sense in small offices in small cities where there weren't many architects. Deac could keep his employees, and I could keep a job when there wasn't much work. I shared his risk. He shared his profits.

Unfortunately, in big firms in big cities with big labor markets, you can't cut that deal. People won't join you for two-thirds salary and an iffy bonus. You can't ask your employees to share the risk. Bonuses are extra. They go on top of the going rate.

Profit incentive? Right. The idea is simple: If you return some of the profits to people who help earn them, they will want to make more profits. If you pay a bonus when there is no profit, it will become expected compensation rather than profit sharing. It will lose its incentive.

Who gets bonuses?

To the extent possible, you want to run the company with automatic mechanisms that reward people for supporting company goals. Tying bonuses to profits does that. But profit incentives don't work for everyone, because not everyone controls profits.

I've heard people argue that because everyone does work that creates profits, everyone should receive bonuses. Yes, everybody's actions affect the company's performance. However, few employees feel that they have much effect on profits. They don't have profit-and-loss responsibility and don't see financial reports. The smell of profit just isn't there. Most employees feel their contributions are pretty diluted.

Bonuses are more meaningful if they are restricted to people with direct profit-and-loss responsibility—people who have high-risk or high-control positions or who have a significant effect on the firm's performance.

The smaller the group being measured, the more individuals feel they can affect results. Conversely, if individual contributions are minor, incentive is lost. Take it to the extreme: If your efforts were rewarded on the basis of a rise in the gross national product, you might not feel you had much chance of affecting results.

Profit centers must live in the real business world; they cannot be fabricated. I've seen some managers err by rewarding a staff department manager on some fictitious "profit" that actually represents a savings in a negotiated budget. It doesn't work. Incentive bonuses that reward for performance above a negotiated goal produce good negotiators, not good performers.

The down side

There are a host of potential problems associated with profit-related bonuses. Here are some I have managed to identify:

Short-term results. A group manager can best improve profits—and thus increase bonus money—in the short term by cutting marketing and production costs or avoiding investment in some start-up operation. But that may cut down sales and quality and reduce future growth.

Tunnel vision. When several groups collaborate to produce a service for a client, there are counterproductive internal tensions over division of income—income on which bonuses will be based.

The most valuable people waste their time bickering, and they cause unnecessary accounting costs. Similarly, group leaders encounter situations where they must choose between the good of their group and the good of the company.

Compensation chaos. If your bonuses are based on profits, there may be some big winners or some imbalances in a given year. Most executives worry about that. They are a lot more comfortable when pay level and organizational levels are consistent. And some presidents and chairmen really get upset when a group leader makes more than they do.

If you decide to reward group leaders on the basis of profits, you and the group managers must accept the possibility that profits may produce wide swings in results from one year to the next.

When I was president of CM Inc., a CRS Group subsidiary, we began to produce some spectacular profits. One year my salary and bonus exceeded that of Bill Caudill, the chairman of CRS. Bill, a great mentor of young entrepreneurs, led the cheering. That probably had something to do with our continued good profits. I remembered that well when the chairman and president of one of 3D/I's subsidiaries received a higher bonus than mine.

It's not necessarily the position that counts, but the performance. In 1930, a journalist asked Babe Ruth if he thought it was right that he was paid more than the president of the United States. Ruth thought for a moment and then replied, "*Well, I had a better year than he did.*"

Some people think that bonuses should have a cap to prevent an imbalance if someone is spectacularly successful. How can you believe in incentive compensation and want to cap the incentive?

The up side

The best policy is to have fewer and larger bonuses. Here's why.

Substantial bonuses help keep essential people. With a few key people, you could re-create your company if necessary. These are the people who could be successful in any firm—and the way to keep them in yours is by sharing significant profits with them. Spreading profits too thin makes their bonuses insignificant.

High performers look for big carrots. A classmate of mine stumbled onto the payroll list of the company he worked for. He quit architecture. He later told me: "*Those guys make peanuts. I wouldn't mind paltry pay if I thought there were big bucks later on.*" High performers want a chance at the brass ring. Those who have confidence in their future will look at the rewards waiting for them at the top. They will be encouraged to stay and work hard only if they know the carrot is there.

Widespread, small bonuses are the most expensive of all. Go ahead. Pass out a lot of small bonuses to everyone. It will feel wonderful. Then look at how much you have left over for those who really made things happen. Small bonuses don't keep employees. The appreciation wears off as soon as they're spent. Employees won't remember them a month later when they are offered a job elsewhere.

Don't give frequent bonuses, either. Employees tend to adjust their standard of living based on frequent bonuses. Then they will bitch like hell when the bonus is not there. Annual bonuses are about right.

Significant bonuses provide profit incentive. Only a small percentage of people actually watch and control profits. If their bonus potential is a large percent of their base salary, they have a strong incentive to control costs. You won't have to put pressure on managers; they'll put it on themselves.

OWNERSHIP

Ownership is rewarding not only financially, but culturally. It's the ultimate form of compensation.

The question of ownership doesn't come up in many organizations. Who owns the Metropolitan Museum of Art, the navy, Harvard University, the Department of Public Works? I guess there are owners, but it's not much of an issue to the employees.

In the private sector, ownership is a big issue. Ownership in a growing, profitable company is ownership in a money-making machine: rights to future cash flows and appreciating equity. Enough ownership means control of the company. In a brainpower company, ownership usually implies corporate status; it means belonging to a group—in the social meaning of the word "partner" rather than "stockholder" or "investor."

So ownership can be a far greater motivator than any other kind of compensation. And, consequently, distributing ownership carries all sorts of corporate cultural baggage. If salary, bonuses, and perks are troubling, distributing ownership can wreak havoc.

There are three common issues.

1. Who gets ownership, why, and how?

2. What is the right form of ownership?

3. How is the price of ownership measured?

Who gets ownership, why, and how?

Who? In small companies leadership, control, and ownership are all typically vested in the same people. If bonuses should be restricted to those who control the profits of the company, ownership should be restricted even further—to those who are chosen to join the establishment that runs the company. New owners become leaders, and leaders must share goals, or the leadership pulls in different directions.

But ownership changes more slowly than management needs—and management ability. As companies grow, management and ownership must eventually become disengaged from each other.

Why? Ownership must be transferred if the company is to survive beyond the careers of its founders—and if the founders are to realize the value of the company they created. Furthermore, ownership in the right hands is an incentive: It attracts and keeps good people. And it motivates them to act in the company's interest.

But it only motivates people who feel that they can have some measure of control. In small companies a large percentage of the employees may have a sense of control—and may own a significant portion of the company. In large companies where ownership and management have been separated, smaller amounts of ownership spread among more people carry a smaller sense of proprietorship for an average employee. Ownership becomes simply an investment. But for the leaders it is still the major estate-building part of compensation—and still a powerful motivational force.

How? Ownership can be passed to a small group of future leaders, a large group of employees, the public in a public offering. Or the company can be sold and ownership can pass to another company.

Unless a company has employees who are independently wealthy, the only way ownership can be passed to current employees chosen as future leaders is to give it to them as part of their compensation.

That creates a problem. Typically the future generation is a group of young men and women who are at that time of life when their personal costs are the highest. They are paying for cars, houses, children's education, and they have little income-producing savings or investments. Stock awards in the place of other income are painful. And even outright gifts of stock on top of existing income are a cost burden because the IRS says a stock award is taxable income.

Meanwhile, many founders feel that they've worked hard to build the value of the company and don't think it's fair to give it away. Yet if the basic value of the ongoing business is to be realized, they must pass the baton. For a company to grow, to outlive its founders, indeed, for the founders to realize the value they've created, a long-range program to transfer ownership must be institutionalized. That program can attract and hold future leaders who can add to the value of the founders' stake.

I remember a conversation with Bill Caudill many years ago when I was first made a partner of CRS. He said, "*Chuck, every year I've owned less of CRS—and made more money from it.*"

Distributing ownership is a win-win proposition when it finds the balance between respecting the precious value of equity and recognizing the need to bestow it on future leaders. Eventually CRS went public—sold ownership in the public markets—and reaped significant value for its owners.

But CRS couldn't have done it without first building a broad base of management that gave public investors confidence in its stability. And even after going public, CRS maintained stock incentive programs for future leaders.

In young, small brainpower companies equity is usually kept low—only enough to cover working capital needs. Profits are distributed to the owners through salary and bonuses. But unless the company is to be sold to the public or another company, that practice will have to stop. If the company is to survive, it will eventually have to retain equity to finance ownership transition.

What forms of ownership are appropriate?

There are proprietorships, partnerships, and corporations.

If one person takes a job and assumes its cost, liability, and profit, the business is a proprietorship. If two or more do the same, the business is a partnership. Unlike a proprietorship or partnership, a corporation is an entity separate from the estate of its owners. The corporation, *not its owners*, assumes the cost, liability, and profit. If the corporation fails, the shareholders lose their investment, but their personal assets aren't at risk—theoretically.

There are several kinds of corporations. A "closely-held" corporation has stock that is restricted to a limited group. When ownership is more broadly held, SEC regulations govern the behavior of the company toward its shareholders.

Subchapter S corporations tax ownership as a partnership. A company issuing stock for trade in public markets is a "public" corporation and is subject to more SEC laws and regulations.

Brainpower organizations didn't invent any of these forms of ownership. They have simply adapted to these traditional forms of ownership. And the cultural and operational differences between these legal structures are less than most people think. It is neither the legal structure of ownership nor the accounting procedures that give the company its culture, determine the distribution of ownership, or produce success. I've had to bite my tongue listening to those who have experienced only one form of ownership.

I've been a proprietor, partner, president of a closely-held corporation, and president of a public company. I am neither a lawyer nor an accountant (and you need the best of both before making decisions about legal and accounting issues), but here are thoughts from my own experience and observations that may illustrate some of the differences and similarities.

Partnerships versus corporations. The conventional wisdom is that partnerships will pay less tax and that corporations will limit liability. It's never that simple.

In a proprietorship, a partnership, or a Subchapter S corporation the profits (or losses) are taxed as personal income by the IRS. In other corporations the profits are taxed at the corporate level. And if dividends are distributed to the shareholders, they're taxed again. Theoretically, a corporation has an additional level of taxation.

It doesn't usually work that way. In a closely-held corporation the shareholders are usually the top management. So most of these companies distribute profits in the form of bonuses to management; dividends are not paid. Since bonuses are a pretax expense, the only taxation is at the personal level—unless the IRS finds that the bonuses are directly proportionate to ownership. In that case the IRS will hold that the bonuses aren't really bonuses but a distribution of equity that must be taxed as dividends.

Liability is the other common issue when differentiating between partnerships and corporations. Partners are personally liable for the actions of their company and their partners. Theoretically, corporate shareholders have only their investment at risk. However, the corporate veil isn't bulletproof. Our litigious society has held directors or top management personally responsible for acts of negligence. And most banks require personal guarantees from top management when lending money to closely-held corporations.

So, in practice, the tax and liability differences between closely-held corporations and partnerships blend into shades of gray.

Public versus private corporations. There are also shades of gray between public and private corporations.

When a company becomes public, the vehicle for big rewards changes. In a public corporation management and staff are paid appropriate salaries and bonuses, but the profits are usually retained or reinvested to increase earnings and stock price. Dividends, if they exist at all, are minimal. Big rewards for shareholders come when the price of the stock is driven up by earnings. But when the stock is sold, the IRS takes its share in the form of capital gains tax—so the second level of tax kicks in.

I've heard the claim that public-company managers are pressured to sacrifice long-range goals to produce quarterly results. That could be true, but I've often heard "long-range goals" used as an excuse to avoid tough cost-control decisions in a downturn. I recall a quotation attributed to John Maynard Keynes: "*I never worry about the long run, because in the long run we'll all be dead.*"

I've heard owners of private companies say, "*We don't have to produce a profit to keep shareholders happy, so we can do better work—we can stress quality.*" That's silly. Public companies have to produce quality or they'll go out of business. The pressure to produce profit is a good pressure—public or private.

Owners of private companies may be inclined to manage their companies to serve their personal goals and are criticized accordingly by the managers of public companies. Sometimes this is less criticism than envy. Personal goals may reflect high professional aspirations. And public companies aren't free of self-interest. It's true that many private companies buy airplanes and hunting lodges because that's what the owners want. But a little observation shows how many jets on the private aviation ramp are owned by public companies. And the fanciest hunting lodge I ever visited was owned by a public company.

Theoretically, the managers of public companies have the stockholders' interest—return on investment—as their first responsibility. But despite the theory that stockholders have control of a public company, most stockholders don't understand the business they've invested in; they give their proxies to management. They simply buy and sell stock based on the performance of one company or another. Most public companies have deeply entrenched managers who run the companies as they see fit. The stockholders' only choice is to hold the stock or sell.

The primary motivation behind public ownership of a company is to raise capital—and there's less need for capital in a professional service company than in a smokestack company. But there are valid reasons for a professional service company to go public.

First, it's a means for owners to get their money out. The way to make big bucks is to buy in at equity (or to start a company that becomes big and profitable) and sell at a multiple of earnings—to the public or another company. People who can build money-making machines make a lot of money.

Second, public ownership puts a market value on stock, which obviates the need for troublesome buy/sell agreements among the company's owners. It also provides currency for acquisition of other companies or capital for growth-minded executives who want to fund expansion.

But there are also advantages in keeping a company private. Private companies avoid the cost and distraction that go into SEC reports, annual and quarterly reports, and stockholder meetings.

ESOPs. Employee Stock Ownership Plans offer an alternative that many firms have chosen. An ESOP is a trust formed to buy all or part of a company's stock. It may borrow money from a bank to buy the stock and use the stock as security. Typically the debt is guaranteed by the company. The banks get a tax break on ESOP loans, so they pass it on as a lower interest rate. There are also tax breaks to sellers. The note is repaid by the company making contributions to the ESOP (which are tax deductible to the company). All, or a large portion, of the employees vest in the ESOP, and thus in ownership, based on criteria such as salary or length of employment.

Carl M. Sapers, an attorney at Hill & Barlow in Boston and a professor at the Harvard Graduate School of Design, is an expert on ESOPs. He has been counsel to more than fifty architectural firms. He wrote the opinions for both CRS and 3D/I when, a few months apart, they pioneered the idea that an architectural firm could go public.

He explains the advantages of ESOPs as follows:

"ESOPs are an alternative to going public because they afford an opportunity for shareholders who have built a firm to cash in on some of its economic value in much the same way that they could if the company 'went public.' Various tax incentives, including below-market interest rates for leveraging the purchase and long-term deferral of any capital gain, have persuaded many that the ESOP permits you to 'have your cake and eat it, too.' Going public involves bringing in outsiders, running substantial risks as to the ultimate control of the board of directors, and incurring major additional responsibilities under the Securities Acts. The ESOP has none of these negatives."

How is ownership valued?

If a company is publicly held, shares are bought or sold based on their market value—which is set daily by the marketplace. But if a company is private, the shareholders (or partners) typically set rules that restrict the ownership to key employees or special outside investors. Since ownership implies a measure of management control, the company's leaders want to control who owns shares. They need a buy/sell agreement among shareholders that governs the transfer of ownership.

The most important and the most perplexing part of a buy/sell agreement is the troublesome article that sets the price of the shares when they're bought and sold. Setting the price of the shares sets the value of the company. There are books on how to do that—and none of them agree. All you have to do is watch the stock market jump up and down to recognize that nobody knows what companies are really worth.

There are, however, several common approaches that are used—independently or in combination.

Equity. Many buy/sell agreements simply use equity—"book value"—as a means of establishing value. The argument is simple: Subtract liabilities from assets and you have the profits that have been left in the company—the "net worth." That then is the debt that the company owes the shareholders. So if a shareholder leaves the company, the shareholder gets a pro rata share.

Multiple of earnings. A logical argument is that a company is a money-making machine, and the value of a money-making machine should be determined by how much it can make and how fast it can do it. If a machine makes $100 a year, it might be worth $1,000 to someone who would be happy with a 10 percent return on investment. So the value of a company is the earnings, not the equity.

A professional service company with revenues of $1,000,000 could have equity of $100,000 and a profit of $100,000. That's a 100 percent return on equity! I doubt if the owners of a money machine that produced that kind of return would be very interested in selling shares for the equity price. Furthermore, the company might be growing, so increased future earnings are a large consideration.

But there's a problem. Who knows what next year's earnings will be?

Other multiples. Some formulas that determine stock price for a buy/sell agreement take a percentage of backlog and add it to the equity. The argument is that the owners were there when the work was sold, and the profit to be made on the work under contract should be added to the company's value. The counter argument is that the profit hasn't yet been realized and shouldn't be included.

Other formulas use a multiple of gross revenues to determine stock value. And while it's a common approach, the logic escapes me. A company can lose money on its fees, and losses aren't an asset; they are a *liability*.

Periodic shareholder evaluation. Some companies set the stock value at periodic board or shareholder meetings. The theory is that there are many variables that can be considered and these people know the company's condition. They can make routine judgments and set an equitable price. The problem is that the people who might want to leave the company and sell their stock think of all the reasons it should be priced high and the people who want to stay and buy the stock think of all the reasons it should be priced low.

An opinion. For a closely-held company owned by its leaders, with internal transition programs, I favor setting stock price at equity. Sure, the company may be worth a lot more, but that's not the point.

In a capital-intensive company, the value may be based on assets that have potential future income (such as oil in the ground or appreciated real estate). The shareholders may be completely divorced from leadership.

But for a private company that sells brainpower, it's the leaders who are creating the income. If some leaders leave, they quit producing the future cash flows that create the company's value. Paying them a price that considers future growth and profit is unfair to those who stay. And pricing the stock high gives leaders a reason to leave and cash out rather that stay and continue to create value.

Valuing the stock at equity creates a low price that makes it easy for promising new leaders to "buy in" and participate in the equity they're helping to build. If a stock award program is implemented, setting the price high will increase the tax burden on the recipients of the award. Priced at equity, ownership becomes a prize— something to be treasured. An opportunity to be a shareholder is a reward for excellence and performance, not just an investment.

Valuing a stock at equity helps ensure the future. When the company values stock above equity, there's a leveraged drain on equity when shareholders leave, and protecting equity is prerequisite to a company's longevity. I've seen companies that valued stock above equity—at a multiple of earnings, backlog, revenue, or some other formula—that bought out a major shareholder and found themselves with a negative equity. They became insolvent and simply couldn't stay in business. Or the existing shareholders had to dip into their savings to recapitalize the company.

Yet there are times, even in closely-held brainpower companies, when it's proper to consider a stock price above equity. One common time is when a long-term leader retires. At that point it's only fair to consider the value of what that leader has created for those who inherit the firm. Putting a multiple on the stock is one solution. An alternative is to continue to value the stock at equity and add special retirement benefits.

And there should be special considerations when there are assets (such as an office building or other investments) with appreciated values that aren't reflected in the balance sheet.

Other times when the stock of a small brainpower company might well be valued above equity are when it is sold or when an outside investor is brought in to finance significant growth.

No solution. Finally, the company is worth what the shareholders agree they will buy and sell it for. There's no formula that will measure the true value of a company. It's worth a lot more in years of high growth and profit than in periods of decline and loss. A company that shows a loss and has spent its profits in promising new technology or in promising new starts in growth markets is worth more than a company that ekes out a small profit in a dying market. A company that has dynamic new leadership is worth more than one that has lost its leadership no matter what the current profits are. And 51 percent of the company is worth a whole lot more than 49 percent.

The true value of a company depends on the future cash flows it produces for its shareholders—what it will ultimately bring to its owners in the way of hard cash. Since that's a future event, the value is based on one's guess of what the future will bring.

CHAPTER 2

Scoreboards

The usual problems with financial reporting systems are too much information, accounting formats that don't fit the company structure, and misleading precision.

COMMON FLAWS

Flaw 1: Management information systems produce too much information

Computers can massage and regurgitate data so easily that you can produce a different report for everyone. The result: Vital facts are buried in trivia. We are flooded with "interesting" information and waste time filling out and reading trivial reports.

Most reporting systems produce too much paper. Vital information is scattered and diffused. Reports should be designed to get the most relevant facts on one page. Consider financial data as a mosaic. If you look at the tiles one by one, you never understand the whole picture.

Flaw 2: Accounting formats don't fit management structures

Accounting is a beautifully conceived discipline, and the balance sheet is an invention second only to the wheel. But too often the wheel doesn't fit the wagon. Financial information is presented in categories that don't reflect management responsibilities. Managers look at the numbers and celebrate or grieve but have no control over what they see.

Let me illustrate. Say you have several groups and each group leader is responsible for marketing. You first measure the income and expense of each group. Then you take marketing man-hours off the time sheets from all groups, add them up, and enter the total marketing cost on one line on your profit and loss report. You know how much you are spending on marketing, but no one knows who's managing it. There is no accountability in the accounting.

If you give people the responsibility for managing a cost, you have to tell them what they are spending. They need feedback to keep their expenses in line.

The idea of matching categories to responsible managers sounds obvious, but in the process of investigating possible acquisitions I've looked at a lot of financial reports. Very few reported costs in accounts that matched the structure of management authority. Too often income and expense are categorized into traditional accounts that have little to do with the way the company operates.

Managers can't be held accountable for costs they don't manage. But if expenses are organized around management responsibilities, then managers know how much they are spending—and so does the boss. Organizing accounting that way isn't hard, but it's usually neglected.

Flaw 3: The precision of the process exceeds the accuracy of the assumptions

Accounting and management information systems aren't precise. For example, if you keep books on a cash basis, you may get some big payments one month and none the next. Accrual accounting is designed to solve that problem: to match income and expense to a given reporting period (usually a month). But even with accrual accounting, reports are inevitably misleading. Consider the three fundamental entries of income, expense, and equity.

1. Income. In accrual accounting, you have to use some consistent logic to determine how much money you are making each month. Some firms simply add up all the bills for services that they send out on the first of the month and then make adjustments for "fee billed unearned" and "fee earned unbilled." Others use the "percent complete" method and multiply the total fee times a "percent complete." If they are 50 percent complete, they score as "earned fee" 50 percent of the total fee. They decide that this is the income, whether they have billed all or none of the fee. However 50 percent is only a guess, and we all know how often we miss those guesses. Harper and Shuman have written the accounting program most commonly used by AE firms. Neil Harper tells me that he has developed twenty different methods of recognizing income and every new client wants him to develop another.

2. Expense. The depreciation of buildings and equipment proceeds at fixed rates that may bear little relationship to replacement or market value. Buildings may actually be appreciating, while equipment may be worthless to anyone but you the day after you buy it. And if the useful life matches the depreciation life, it is only a coincidence.

3. Stockholders' equity. On a balance sheet, equity is the difference between a firm's assets and its liabilities. But that difference doesn't really report what the company is worth. A company is a money-making machine. The value of a money-making machine isn't what it costs to make. Its value is a function of how much money it *can* make.

Consider this analogy. Say I have a machine that makes $100 a year. I might be able to sell it for $1,000 because that would give the buyer a 10 percent return on investment per year. If the buyer thought it would wear out in a few years, though, it'd be worth less. If the buyer thought it could run faster and make more as time goes by, it'd be worth more.

Equity doesn't reveal a company's worth. It only states how much is left after you subtract other liabilities from assets.

THE BALANCE SHEET

The purpose of a balance sheet is to state the financial condition of an organization at a given point in time.

You have to understand the structure of balance sheets and profit and loss statements so that you can decide how these financial reports should be structured to explain the company most clearly. They are simple, but most professionals never develop a good understanding of even basic financial reports. I was well into my forties before I learned how to read a balance sheet and understand its clear, elegant logic.

The categories are far from universal. There is no accepted dictionary or glossary with agreed-upon, precise definitions. Words like *backlog*, *fixed assets*, *sales*, *fee*, and *profit* have widely different meanings to accountants and their clients. The formats and approach on the following pages are oriented to a corporation, not a partnership, but the principles and issues are universal.

The balance sheet is a picture of the company's financial condition, frozen at one instant in time. It is a financial snapshot. Balance sheets are more important to capital-intensive companies than to labor-intensive companies. Industry uses money to make money. Investments in plant and equipment, resources (such as oil in the ground), raw material, and inventories are all assets with the potential to be turned into future cash flows.

In a company that sells professional services, the assets are brains. Brains produce future cash flows. You can't measure brains on a balance sheet, so balance sheets are less important. But that doesn't mean they are useless. They can tell you how much you have invested in the company and provide indicators of the company's financial health.

See pages 66 and 67 for a sample balance sheet for a hypothetical company.

The structure of every balance sheet is symmetrical; the assets column is on the left, the liabilities-and-equity column is on the right, and one side always adds up to equal the other. Here's my way of looking at the items and watching over them.

1. Assets. Assets are listed in order of their probable liquidity. Current assets are items such as cash and equivalents, accounts receivable, fee earned unbilled, notes receivable, and prepaid expenses. They are called "current" because they may be converted to cash in approximately a year or less.

2. Cash and equivalents. There is no more comforting entry on a balance sheet—and probably none more accurate—than cash. Cash equivalents are such items as certificates of deposit or bonds that may be readily turned into cash. A shortage of cash will force a company to make all kinds of expensive decisions to keep operating. It will lease equipment at rates higher than its own return on investment, it will be forced to make conservative marketing decisions, and it won't have the means to grasp opportunities.

3. Accounts receivable. Usually a professional service company's largest asset is its accounts receivable. It is often overstated. Too many firms carry ARs as assets when they are in fact uncollectable bad debts.

4. Doubtful accounts. Some of your clients won't pay you; it's inevitable. You need to subtract money to cover bad debts. Some companies squirrel away bad debts in one lump sum when they learn that they are uncollectable. But that causes gyrations in apparent earnings and upsets everything you try to accomplish with accrual accounting. You can't really know how well the company is doing because of that extraordinary write-off. It is better to review your ARs in detail and decide what portion you might not collect. Then set aside a percentage of your earned fee every month to keep the total adequate.

Doubtful accounts are a liability, but the convention is to show them as a negative asset immediately under the ARs so the two numbers can be compared easily.

5. Fee earned unbilled. Assume a contract says that you can't bill till you've received approval for a specific phase of the work. Nevertheless, you worked on the project this month, and you figure that you earned something. The work you

1. ASSETS

2.	Cash and equivalents	250,000	8%
3.	Accounts receivable	1,600,000	51%
4.	Doubtful accounts	(200,000)	−6%
5.	Fee earned unbilled	200,000	6%
6.	Investment in JVs	100,000	3%
7.	Prepaid expenses	120,000	4%
8.	Other current assets	50,000	2%
9.	Total current assets	2,120,000	67%
10.	Furnishings & equipment	220,000	7%
11.	Leasehold improvements	200,000	6%
12.	Real estate	500,000	16%
13.	Other long-term assets	120,000	4%
14.	Total long-term assets	1,040,000	33%
15.	TOTAL ASSETS	$3,160,000	100%

16. LIABILITIES

17.	Short-term debt	147,400	5%
18.	Current long-term debt	80,000	3%
19.	Accounts payable	278,000	9%
20.	Fee billed unearned	216,000	7%
21.	Other current liabilities	130,000	4%
22.	Deferred income tax	936,000	30%
23.	Total current liabilities	1,787,400	27%
24.	Long-term debt	162,000	5%
25.	Other long-term liabilities	324,000	10%
26.	Total long-term liabilities	486,000	15%
27.	Total liabilities	2,273,400	72%
28.	Stockholders' equity	886,600	28%
29.	TOTAL LIABILITIES AND EQUITY	$3,160,000	100%

30. INDICATORS

31.	Working capital	$332,000
32.	Current ratio	1.19
33.	Return on equity	10%

did is an asset. It has value. The "earned unbilled" category allows you to record income for the effort you have put out and for which you will soon be able to bill.

As with ARs, this entry is usually inflated. It is too easy to believe that you're 90 percent complete instead of 70 percent. I've seen a lot of projects that were right on projection until the last 10 percent. Then it turned out we needed another 20 percent to finish.

As long as the company is running at a steady state, an overstated "earned unbilled" entry probably won't be too bad. It goes unnoticed because projects in the early, overstated phases are offset by other projects in the late phases where the additional unscheduled man-hours are being expended to finish the work. These are compensating errors.

But in periods of growth, there are more projects in early phases. Therefore, a higher percentage of projects have overstated income. Profits are overstated.

And in periods of decline more projects are finishing. Overruns rear their ugly heads. Previously declared profits have to be compensated by current losses. One more set of woes plagues the poor managers who are already cutting staff and dealing with the other agonies of a declining business.

In every company I've worked for, and in every acquisition I've seen, "earned unbilled" has been overstated. It's not cheating; it's just that we all believe we can finish our projects more easily than we really can. It's a fact of life. When it comes to estimating work to be done, there are more optimists than pessimists .

There are ways to deal with the problem: Hold back a contingency that can be used to finish the job after all the fee has been used up, or record earnings into "fee billed unearned" as labor and expense only—without profit, perhaps even without overhead! Both of these techniques seem silly, but to ignore the fact that people always overestimate percent complete is even sillier.

6. Investment in joint ventures. Often we get together with other firms to do a job. We both sign the contract and are "jointly and severally responsible." We are a joint venture—a new business entity. Then we open a JV bank account, and it has undisbursed funds in it. Part of it is our money; we just don't have it in our own accounts.

Frankly, it's unnecessary to have these JV accounts. It's better to simply let one firm bill the client and pay the other firm for its services. But for some silly reason, a lot of professionals think that a JV has to have a bank account. They can't possibly let a partner touch their money, no matter how much it improves the cash flow. Silly. Nothing uses up useful cash more uselessly than a lot of bank accounts.

7. Prepaid expenses. Say that today you paid for insurance for the next twelve months. You have the value of that coverage that you don't have to pay for again until next year. That is a current asset. It reduces the need for future expenditures.

Why would you want to pay for something before you have to? Two reasons: First, you may get a discount. Second, many companies pay taxes on a cash, rather than accrual, basis. These companies prepay items, such as insurance, rent, or consultants' fees, just before the end of their fiscal year to reduce cash profits and, therefore, taxes.

8. Other current assets. "Other" might include travel advances to employees or various kinds of short-term employee debt to the company.

9. Total current assets. Current assets are those that can be turned into cash (or negate the need to spend cash) within a year. You should have a subtotal for current assets so you can compare your current assets to your current liabilities— the liabilities you will need to pay for in cash within a year.

It's a straightforward concept. If all of your assets get tied up, you might get yourself in a cash flow bind. So you need to know what current assets you can turn into cash and what *current liabilities* you have that will require cash.

10. Furnishings, fixtures, and equipment (FF&E). FF&E is a long-term asset. Once you've bought FF&E, you generally don't need to spend more money. And you have their value working for you. You depreciate these assets a little every month until the asset reaches zero. These items can be tricky. Although they have value to you, they may not have value to others. If you decide to shut down an office and have no buyer for the furnishings, you may take an abrupt write-off. An asset may evaporate into thin air. Consequently, banks don't generally consider these kinds of long-term assets as good collateral for loans.

11. Leasehold improvements. If you rent space, it's unlikely that anyone will ever want to pay you much for your leasehold improvements, any more than they'll want to pay you much for your used FF&E. They have value to you, though, and they will for as long as you're in business.

12. Real estate. If you own your own office building, you insert the cost here—not the market value.

This number can be misleading. On one balance sheet, I remember the depreciated value of an office building entered at $750,000 when the land it was on had appreciated to a market value of $6,000,000: an understatement of 800 percent! But that's GAAP, the generally accepted accounting principles.

You would think that the opposite might apply, but it doesn't. Accounting principles guide you to recognize a loss when you believe it is probable but not recognize a gain until it has been realized. Thus, if the market value of real estate increases, you shouldn't record the increase on your balance sheet until you sell it and prove it. Conversely, if the market value decreases, you should record the deflated value. But there is a world of real estate on balance sheets that still carries the purchase price after the bottom has dropped out of the market.

These rules are not without logic. Cost-less-depreciation is a consistent entry; any other number is speculation. If you want consistent reports, you can't speculate on value every month. But inflation of real estate values can wreak havoc with balance sheets. Because of these discrepancies, some people have two balance sheets: the cost-basis balance sheet based on the rules and another balance sheet based on estimates or appraisals of today's market values.

What a balance sheet reveals is relevant; what it conceals is crucial. It's an inexact science. You have to know what's behind the numbers to make sense of it all.

13. Other long-term assets. There is always a category called "other" or "miscellaneous." When it gets to be the biggest number on the list, it's time to break it down into more categories.

14. Total long-term assets. Unless you make a major purchase—say, of computers, furniture, or a building—these numbers remain fairly stable. They decline as items are depreciated and increase as new items are purchased. Real estate varies: Buildings depreciate, land doesn't. Since these items are hard to turn into cash, bankers don't like to consider them when they lend money—unless it's in the form of a mortgage loan that amortizes over a longer period of time.

15. Total assets. For a company selling brain-power, assets are not necessarily good. It depends on the form these assets take. Cash is good, but accounts receivable are always a problem. FF&E and leasehold improvements mean future depreciation costs. If you collect your ARs, you might pay bonuses and increase cash and equivalents. The result: fewer assets and more cash for liquidity.

16. Liabilities. Assets are listed *in order of their probable liquidity*. Ergo, liabilities are listed *in order of their priority of demand on liquidity*. Accounts payable, short-term debt, fee billed but unearned, long-term debt, and stockholders' equity are examples of the descending priority of claim upon the assets.

17. Short-term debt. If you borrow money that must be repaid in a year, it is short-term debt. The most common use of short-term debt is to finance accounts receivable.

Most professional service companies pay taxes on a cash basis rather than an accrual basis. They keep two sets of books. The accrual set records ARs as income and thus matches income and expense for each month. The cash set records income only when payment is received. Earnings appear erratic, but taxes do not have to be paid on uncollected ARs.

It's common practice for cash-basis businesses to delay some bills and prepay some expenses in the last month of their fiscal year to defer taxes. They may then have to borrow to cover operating expenses until the bills can be collected and the benefit of the prepaid expenses is realized. The ARs grow since invoices for work performed were not mailed.

18. Current portion of long-term debt. Most long-term debts have periodic payments. If a note to a retired stockholder has an annual installment or if a mortgage has monthly payments, the portion that must be paid in the next year is the "current portion of long-term debt."

19. Accounts payable. Most of us pay our bills faster than our clients pay us. Compare this entry—the money you owe—to the accounts receivable if you want to remind yourself that life isn't fair.

20. Fee billed unearned. Fee billed unearned is the opposite of fee earned unbilled. If your fees are front-end loaded or if you get a down payment before you start work, you enter the unearned portion here. It is entered on the liability side of the balance sheet because you are liable for the work. It's like a loan from a client—you haven't earned it yet.

The down payment increases your cash assets so you need an offsetting liability until you do the work. When the work is done, the fee billed unearned is depleted, and, assuming you make a profit, this profit reappears as cash and stockholders' equity—an asset and a liability. The balance sheet stays in balance. Fee billed unearned, like stockholders' equity, is a liability that you want.

21. Other current liabilities. These could be debts to clients to settle project problems, vacation days owed to employees, or a host of other possibilities.

22. Deferred income tax. If you pay tax on a cash basis, you should recognize that when you collect your ARs you will have to pay income tax on them. The entry here is the total ARs times your tax rate plus or minus possible adjustments for investment tax credits, taxes on foreign operations, and so on.

I've heard people say, "*That isn't a current liability. As long as we have ARs, we'll have a tax liability.*" Well, you will always have ARs, too. So if you want to call them current, you have to call the tax liability current, too. If you collected all your ARs, you'd have to pay the tax.

Some companies pay tax on the accrual basis— and with tax reform, more companies are under pressure to become accrual taxpayers. When they do so, they'll do their best to convince the IRS that their allowance for doubtful accounts should be increased.

23. Total current liabilities. Current liabilities are those that will probably demand cash within a year. Compare them to current assets so you can determine your probable cash flow demands.

24. Long-term debt. "Long-term" typically means more than one year. It usually covers mortgages on real estate, equipment-purchase loans, and debts to retiring stockholders.

25. Other long-term liabilities. There is always an "other" category. Any good manager will always question what's in it.

26. Total long-term liabilities. The sum of all long-term liabilities.

27. Total liabilities. The sum of all liabilities.

28. Stockholders' equity. Stockholders' equity is often called "book value." Why is equity on the liability side of the balance sheet? Because it's the debt the company owes to its owners. The stockholders have a claim on whatever is left after all other liabilities have been satisfied; therefore, the stockholders' equity appears last. Added to the other liabilities, it balances with the assets. Hence the term "balance sheet."

Most professional service companies have buy/sell agreements among their stockholders. If someone leaves, the company is obligated—or at least has the option—to buy the stock. Equity and cash are both reduced (or debt to the ex-shareholder increases long- or short-term debt), so the balance sheet stays in balance.

Many owners of professional service companies find it tough to cash in their stock. They have given profits to themselves and employees as bonuses over the years, and have stayed undercapitalized. Then there are no assets to purchase stock. When a major stockholder leaves, the company suffers a lack of liquidity.

Since the same thing can happen if a stockholder dies, most companies take out key-stockholder insurance, with the company as beneficiary. Then, in the event of a death, there is enough cash to pay off the estate and the company stays liquid. Each surviving stockholder then has a larger share of the same equity.

Stockholder agreements often value the stock of privately held firms at some price above equity. That's often fair, for the same reason the stock market frequently prices public companies far above their book value: The value of a company lies in its ability to make money and in its potential for growth.

It is possible, however, that when stockholders agree that the firm will purchase the stock of stockholders who leave and when that stock is valued above book value, then the book value could become less than zero if a major shareholder were to retire. I've seen it happen, and I think it's wise to have covenants in the stockholders agreement to restrict payments in that eventuality.

29. Total liabilities and equity. The sum of all liabilities and equity. Said in a more logical way, total liabilities subtracted from total assets equals equity.

30. Balance sheet indicators. These are some key ratios that can be important.

31. Working capital. A firm's ability to handle expenses is a function of its liquidity. A rough indicator of liquidity is working capital. If you subtract current liabilities (the money you must soon pay) from current assets (the money you will soon collect), you determine the company's working capital—the theoretical amount of surplus cash you would have if you cashed in all your short-term assets and paid all your short-term liabilities.

32. Current ratio. Another way to gauge liquidity is by the current ratio, calculated by dividing current assets by current liabilities. The current ratio is important: If all of your assets are tied up, you can find yourself in a cash-flow bind and be forced to consider liquidating some of those assets. If so, you'll need to know whether the current assets that you can turn into cash amount to more than the current liabilities that will be demanding your cash. The current ratio tells you how fast you can cover your debts—and the banker you go to for a quick loan to stay in business will want to know that, too.

Brainpower firms typically have lower current ratios than smokestack companies, for two reasons: First, most brainpower firms operate on the assumption that since their major cost is labor, costs can be cut by firing people; in industry, the major costs are the fixed costs of plant, equipment, and inventory. Second, brainpower firm owners tend to think of their companies as producers of income for themselves; they extract cash (and pay taxes) rather than retain earnings. This leaves their firms less able to weather economic downturns.

33. Return on equity. After-tax profits are calculated as a percent return on invested capital (shareholders' equity) to compare with other investment alternatives. Because professional service companies are usually closely held and earnings distributed as bonuses, this common accounting indicator is rarely meaningful.

In the sample balance sheet, a return on equity of 10 percent would require an after-tax profit of $88,600. Ten percent after taxes, after bonuses, after everything else would be very good for a privately held professional service company. Most pay out profits in bonuses. As a matter of fact, many companies consider ownership when they pay bonuses—a kind of "phantom dividend." It is paid as a bonus because a dividend is not tax deductible to the company; a bonus is. Owners are, therefore, careful to make sure that ownership and bonuses are not directly proportional. Otherwise the IRS would claim that they are dividends and collect taxes.

THE PROFIT AND LOSS STATEMENT

In order to make money, you've got to know how much is coming in and how much is going out and make the tough decisions to ensure that there is a difference. The profit and loss statement is the basic control tool for that purpose. It's a summary of income and expenses for a given reporting period—a flow report.

The purpose of a profit and loss statement is to match income and expense for a given period. Think of money as water and think of the firm as a water tank with a pipe that is filling the tank at the top and a drain pipe that is emptying the tank at the bottom. The balance sheet measures how much water the firm has in the tank. The profit and loss statement measures the difference between the rate of flow in and the rate of flow out.

The most important part of the P&L statement is the projection. The projection should cover about three months. Here's why. Assume that business starts to turn down in January. January's financial reports come out in mid-February. Even if you take immediate action, you won't be able to trim costs until March is over; you have just had three bad months. So if you want to manage costs before you have a bad month, you must make good projections of future income and expense—about three months ahead of time.

A good P&L statement outlines income and expense simply, in a clear format that managers will understand.

On pages 82–83 is an example of a P&L statement that I think is properly formatted:

The first step is to determine net earned fee—how much you have to run your business. You can't just use a list of all the bills you are sending your clients. They contain sums you will be paying to subcontractors and such project-related reimbursable expenses as travel and printing—money that runs through your fingers. Subtract these types of expenses and get down to the raw amount of money that is actually available to you.

The second step is to categorize your expenses: how much you need to run your business. Determine the regular expenses of doing business. They are classically broken into two categories— those costs that are incurred in executing work (direct job costs, or DJC) and overhead costs (general and administrative, or G&A).

I've said that in a brainpower company, brains are the biggest asset, and I don't know how to get brains on a balance sheet. But you can measure the cost—the cost of labor. Labor is a raw material. Typically, managers of smokestack companies are sensitive to managing expenses. That's logical. The costs of materials and equipment are their major expenses. But in brainpower companies, people are the major expense. And those people create the other expenses. So if you control labor costs, you control your major expense.

The most sensible structure for a professional service company's P&L report is to itemize costs into two broad categories: labor in the first and everything else in the second. Other reports can break down each category into whatever detail is necessary. Most companies produce too much detail; if you don't have a P&L report simple enough to remember, it's too complicated.

Here are my definitions of P&L terms.

1. Scheduled backlog. This is the work you have and the fees you expect to earn on projects that are under contract and for which you have authorization to proceed.

STATEMENT OF PROFIT AND LOSS

	JAN		FEB		MARCH		THIS MONTH				MAY		JUNE		JULY		Y-T-D AVERAGE	
							FORECAST		ACTUAL									
1 Scheduled backlog	1070	100%	910	100%	870	100%	840	90%	852	88%	940	90%	900	85%	860	78%	956	
2 Expected new sales	0	0%	0	0%	0	0%	92	10%	120	12%	100	10%	155	15%	240	22%		
3 GROSS INCOME	1070	100%	910	100%	870	100%	932	100%	972	100%	1040	100%	1055	100%	1100	100%	956	100%
4 Subcontracts	32	3%	43	5%	35	4%	36	4%	36	4%	29	3%	38	4%	34	3%	37	4%
5 Reimbursable expense	38	4%	42	5%	45	6%	40	5%	40	4%	42	4%	40	4%	39	4%	41	5%
6 NET EARNED FEE	1000	100%	825	100%	790	100%	856	100%	896	100%	969	100%	977	100%	1027	100%	878	100%
7 Direct job labor	310	31%	290	35%	288	36%	290	34%	300	33%	305	31%	318	33%	335	33%	297	34%
8 Direct job expense	44	4%	42	5%	41	5%	50	6%	44	5%	38	4%	41	4%	52	5%	43	5%
9 TOTAL JOB COST	354	35%	332	40%	329	42%	340	40%	344	38%	343	35%	359	37%	387	38%	340	39%
10 CONTRIBUTION TO O&P	646	65%	493	60%	461	58%	516	60%	552	62%	626	65%	618	63%	640	62%	538	61%
11 Marketing labor	40	4%	48	5%	47	5%	50	5%	40	4%	50	5%	50	5%	50	5%	44	4%
12 Marketing expense	20	2%	28	3%	29	3%	20	2%	20	2%	20	2%	20	2%	20	2%	24	2%
13 Management labor	120	12%	132	13%	131	13%	126	13%	129	13%	125	13%	116	12%	125	13%	128	13%
14 Management expense	260	26%	259	26%	266	27%	260	26%	255	26%	260	26%	260	26%	260	26%	260	26%
15 TOTAL OVERHEAD	440	44%	467	47%	473	47%	456	46%	444	44%	455	46%	446	45%	455	46%	456	46%
16 PROFIT (BDDB&T)	206	21%	26	3%	(12)	-2%	60	7%	108	12%	171	18%	172	18%	185	18%	82	9%

INDICATORS

17 MULTIPLES									
18 Labor multiple	3.08	2.70	2.60	2.78	2.84	3.05	2.94	2.91	2.81
19 Break-even multiple	2.42	2.61	2.64	2.57	2.48	2.49	2.40	2.36	2.54
20 PERCENT BILLABLE	66%	62%	62%	62%	64%	64%	66%	66%	63%
21 EMPLOYEE DATA	47%	57%	59%	54%	52%	50%	50%	50%	53%
22 Total labor cost	470	470	466	466	469	480	484	510	469
23 Total employees	131	131	129	129	131	133	134	141	131
24 Average salary	3588	3588	3612	3612	3580	3609	3612	3617	3592
25 % annual increase	4.0%	4.0%	4.7%	4.7%	3.8%	4.6%	4.7%	4.8%	4.1%
26 Earned fee /employee	7634	6298	6124	6636	6840	7286	7291	7284	6724
27 BACKLOG									
28 Hot prospects	8240	9368	8890	8830	9930	6000	8200	7800	9107
29 Awarded/unsigned	2240	1900	2200	1900	1950	2200	2300	2400	2073
30 New backlog (sales)	600	260	970	1000	1840	1000	1000	1000	918
31 Backlog contracted	6800	6235	6415	6559	7359	7390	7413	7386	6702
32 Backlog /employee	52	48	50	51	56	56	55	52	51
33 Backlog turnover	204	227	244	230	246	229	228	216	230
34 ACCOUNTS RECEIVABLE									
35 Current	3321	2900	2500	2500	2700				2855
36 Over 90 days	987	678	746	845	653				766
37 Doubtful	100	87	75	75	81				86
38 Turnover	100	105	95	88	90				98

Sometimes you work on projects under a letter of intent. The client is paying the bills, and you are confident that you have a contract. Perhaps the lawyers are discussing fine print, a board needs to approve the contract, or you are dealing with a trusted repeat client. Most firms include these fees in scheduled backlog. I think that's okay. Nothing in the world is absolutely sure. Even a signed-contract project can be shut down with a phone call.

This top line—scheduled backlog—must be a number that you have confidence in. Like all the numbers that follow, it must reflect judgment.

2. Expected new sales. This is the work you hope to get. If you only forecast scheduled backlog, you'd always be predicting a downturn in business. So you must forecast the amount of fee that you expect to earn from new sales in each of the next few months. This nomenclature is a little misleading; it should read "fee to be earned from work yet to be sold and contracted," but that's a little long.

Expected new sales are transformed into scheduled backlog as contracts are signed. So the number is zero this month and in months past. It becomes increasingly larger in the months ahead. Expected new sales is not a wish list. It should be calculated from projects that are already in the pipeline. In a three-month projection of fees to be earned on work yet to be contracted, there should be little speculation. Projects should be known; schedules for contract execution and project start-ups should be pretty well established. If pie-in-the-sky creeps in, the rest of the exercise is wasted effort.

No matter how analytical you are, both of these numbers are guesses. Some managers tend to be optimistic, others pessimistic. It's wise to correct for each. In periods of downturn, most will over-estimate new sales; in periods of growth, we underestimate.

3. Gross income. This is total earned revenues, including fees, consultants, reimbursables, and markups. Gross income should not include revenue unrelated to your principal line of business (such as real estate investments, interest on outside business activities, or sublease income). If those items exist, they should be at the bottom of the sheet and described as "other" or "extraordinary" income.

4. Subcontracts. These are the costs of outside consultants, joint venture partners, or other subcontractors related to your principal line of business. It does not include temporary contract labor; contract labor costs are included in reimbursable expenses or in direct job expense. Exclude your markup on consultants from this subtraction—if you are clever enough to get any.

5. Reimbursable expenses. These are the expenses reimbursed by the client, typically project-related, nonconsultant expenses such as travel, printing, and long-distance telephone. The logic is this: The company carries little risk if the expense is reimbursable. Again, markups are excluded.

The object here is still to get down to the income available to you to run your firm with its usual expenses. You're trying to take out all those costs that are actually used to run other people's companies. The haggling comes when the printing bill on one project is reimbursable—deducted as a reimbursable expense prior to the net earned fee and included as direct job expense—but included as part of the fixed fee on another project. Theoretically, you have no risk when it's reimbursable and you do have risk when it's part of a lump sum. The fact of the matter is that firms really do have risk on reimbursable expenses; they often overrun a guaranteed maximum or simply don't get paid.

6. Net earned fee. This is the money generated by the firm's services. It isn't total (gross) income; some of that income has been spent on subcontracts and reimbursable expenses. Net earned fee is the money actually available to run the company—and most good managers will watch that number like a hawk and be able to quote it from memory.

7. Direct job labor (DJL). This is the raw labor charged to projects. It should not include fringe benefits such as bonuses, vacation, sick leave, payroll taxes, or nonjob labor, which are all included in overhead. But it should include all nontechnical employee time that can be charged to projects—typing time for specification preparation, for example.

8. Direct job expenses (DJE). These are project-related, nonreimbursable, nonconsultant expenses such as travel, subsistence, printing, and long-distance telephone. They should be clearly broken out because they are expenses that must be carefully managed. When these costs are reduced, the company's profits grow. (Reimbursable expenses must be managed, too, but they do not affect the bottom line unless a maximum limit is specified and exceeded.)

9. Total job cost. This is the sum of direct job labor and direct job expense. Many firms assign overhead to labor costs and mark up total job cost accordingly; for each dollar of project labor cost, dollars and cents of company overhead are added to the project. That's wrong, because project managers discover their project costs loaded with overhead that they can't control. Overhead is the responsibility of top management, and adding its costs to projects dilutes the relative importance of direct job labor and direct job expenses—expenses a project manager should work hard to control. It's far better to report raw cost against a budget. It's preferable to set aside a portion of the fee to do the job and keep a close watch on the project multiple.

10. Contribution to overhead and profit. Sometimes called gross profit, this is the money available to pay for total overhead and profit. It's what is left after labor and expenses required to do the job have been paid. Some projects produce lower contributions than others, usually for good reason: Big projects are often staffed with fully job-chargeable teams, and telephones, office equipment, office space, and accounting and clerical staff are all part of the fee. A large part of overhead on such projects is actually project cost, so a lower contribution is required for the firm to make a profit.

11. Marketing labor. This is the raw labor cost of direct promotion (selling jobs) and indirect promotion (public relations, speeches, and so on). Watch this number; it tends to be a dumping ground for labor when there isn't enough work to be done.

12. Marketing expenses. These are the expenses directly associated with marketing labor.

13. Management labor. A misnomer, this is a catch-all entry. It should reflect the cost of all labor that isn't direct job labor or marketing labor. Obviously, that includes a lot of clerical and other labor that isn't really management, but almost everyone calls it management labor anyway. It should include all fringe benefits on the project-labor salaries of all unassigned technical and nontechnical personnel—holidays, vacation, sick leave, and personal time off. This category, too, can be a dumping ground.

14. Management expenses. These are the expenses associated with management labor. Here most firms make the mistake of breaking down overhead into a million different categories, among them rent, telephone, copying, and legal costs. That's a mistake; the raw data are confusing to senior managers who need to look at the big picture. Only when totals are out of line should managers have to take the next step and review the details.

15. Total overhead. This covers all expenses that can't be assigned to a billable project. Overhead costs are intractable and sluggish. They respond slowly to control. When net earned fee goes up, overhead lags behind; profits are good. But eventually overhead catches up. When net earned fee goes down, overhead lags again, and losses result. Few things are more important in financial management than developing mechanisms to control overhead quickly.

16. Operating profit (BDD & T). These are the total funds available for profits "before discretionary disbursements and taxes." Most companies that sell brainpower control their after-tax profit by paying it out as bonuses. Therefore, profit after discretionary disbursements and taxes is not a meaningful measure of performance. If bonuses are not a committed annual benefit of employment, this figure is the pretax profit to be distributed as management sees fit. If bonuses are a commitment of the company, they should be accrued as a line item under overhead expense, before profit.

The percent figure here measures profit, BDD&T, based on net earned fee. As a result, it bases profit percentage only on your own efforts and not on subcontracts and reimbursable expenses. If you get a markup on subcontracts and reimbursable expenses, it will fall straight to the bottom line and increase profits.

Income and expense indicators

A number of indicators can be used to measure the performance of a company. Following are a few of the most common.

17. Multiples. This is the measure of markup on what you are selling—man-hours. A company that buys and sells products must add a markup to pay for overhead and profit. A high-fashion clothing store may mark up products 200 percent, while a general contractor may mark up construction only 2 percent. But professional service firms buy and sell labor, so they mark up labor. Obviously you have to sell it for more than you buy it. How much more? Most AE companies have to sell labor for about 300 percent of what they pay for it. That makes high-fashion clothing look like a bargain.

18. Labor multiple. This is the ratio of dollars of net earned fee to every dollar of direct job labor (DJL) charged to jobs, excluding direct job expenses (DJE).

The following formula calculates the net labor multiple:

$$\frac{net\ earned\ fee - DJE}{DJL} = labor\ multiple$$

It is most meaningful to deal with a net multiplier that excludes direct job expenses, subcontracts, and reimbursable expenses; it calculates the actual markup you achieve on your job labor. When you use this formula, the trick is to make sure that the earned fees, DJE, and DJL are all for the same period.

The multiple is often used in estimating fees for new jobs. You calculate the raw labor cost required, multiply the result by your direct job labor multiple, then add consultants and estimated direct job expenses to achieve the total fee quoted to the client.

19. Break-even labor multiple. This is the ratio of earned fee to billings at the break-even (no profit, no loss) point. The formula:

$$\frac{total\ expenses - DJE}{DJL} = \frac{break\text{-}even}{multiple}$$

Multiples may be calculated for projects, divisions, or the entire company.

Many executives include the total cost of labor—fringes and all—in the base before applying the project multiple. The American Institute of Architects' standard contract forms reflect that approach. For years, the classic formula for reimbursement on a cost-plus job was 2.5 times direct personnel expense (DPE—the cost of raw salaries plus sick leave, vacations, holidays, and payroll taxes). The fringes typically run 25 to 35 percent of raw salaries, and 1.25 times 2.5 equals 3.125; so a multiple of 3.125 times raw labor is equivalent to a multiple of 2.5 times DPE.

Why would a firm start this calculation with raw labor and then add in some overhead with one factor and other overhead with another factor? Why not do it all at once? First, it's easier to tell clients you're marking up labor two and a half times rather than three times. Second, the DPE factor has fat in it; it's based on the assumption that all of your employees will take all of their sick leave and vacation time—which statistics say they don't. Most clients seem to have figured that little subterfuge out nowadays, so most firms have discontinued its practice.

20. Percent billable. Sometimes called the chargeable ratio, this is the percentage of labor dollars that is charged to projects. More specifically, it is the direct job labor cost divided by total labor cost. A calculation could also be made based on time (hours), but the dollar figure is the meaningful number. The profitability of a firm is influenced by the amount of money it spends on labor to create earnings, as opposed to letting that money earn income in some other way.

There is also the average net ratio, which is calculated by omitting the vacation, sick leave, and holiday labor expense; but that's just spreading trivia.

21. Employee data. This is information on your biggest category of cost—your people. The following five indicators all deal with payroll and numbers of employees. These indicators are vital to watch.

22. Total labor cost. This is total payroll, including the cost of people on vacation and sick leave. It's a good number to remember because it's usually a firm's largest single cost and a driver of many other costs. Control labor, and most other costs will fall into line.

23. Average total employees. This is the number of employees, including principals and part-time equivalents.

24. Average salary. This ratio divides total payroll by the average total employees. In a company that sells brainpower, the cost of salaries is somewhat analogous to the cost of raw material in industry: If the cost of the raw material increases, either productivity must increase or the firm must charge its clients more money.

The average salary is usually increased by staff reductions. When you cut, you tend to cut junior people, those who have been with you the least amount of time. You'll keep your experienced, higher paid people. Consequently, your average salary increases. When you grow, you add people to the bottom and dilute the average.

25. Percent annual increase. This is the percentage of increase in average salary. You must monitor and manage the average salary. Look at last year's payroll and divide it by total employment. Compare it to this year's payroll divided by total employment. If the average salary is increasing faster than the cost of living, you may be driving yourself out of business.

Average salary has to be balanced with some other judgments. If you receive a new research contract that requires you to add a cadre of Ph.D.s, you will have a justifiable increase in average salary. If you get a big job that requires the hiring of a lot of draftsmen and clerks, there will be a big dilution.

26. Earned fee per employee. This ratio divides total net earned fee by average total employees including principals and part-time equivalents. It's a general measure of staff productivity.

The number is influenced by the mix of high- and low-paid employees. Foreign staff project teams will have less overhead burden per employee, but the cost of foreign service premiums (moving, transportation, housing, and so on) will increase the amount of fee that must be billed to support the employee. It is a rough indicator, but it is important. Over the years, it will fluctuate with profits.

27. Backlog. This is the amount of business that you have. There are an infinite number of ways to define backlog; the most important thing is to define it consistently—and conservatively. Here are some appropriate categories for backlog reporting.

28. Hot prospects. This is the fee volume on current opportunities. It is a wish list and not worth a lot because most of us believe our chances are better than they really are. Use it if you want, but don't fool yourself.

29. Awarded unsigned. This represents work in the pipeline. It's the total of all fees for projects that have been awarded but not yet turned into negotiated contracts, signed contracts, or active projects. Don't let these anticipated fees get mixed up with the hard numbers in contracted backlog. Looking at what's in the pipeline is wise because it prompts action—at least when the number is low.

30. New backlog (sales). This is the total amount of fees contracted for the current month. For future months, the projected new backlog figures will come from a firm's marketing plan or from the best estimates of marketing and top management.

31. Backlog contracted. This is the total unbilled fees left in the signed contracts that you are currently authorized to work on. It is the business you have in hand.

Most projects have phases with approval points. For some, these approvals are perfunctory, and it's proper to assume that the project will keep moving. For others, the ends of these phases produce reports that are used for go/no-go decisions. Active contracted backlog shouldn't include fees for downstream phases of questionable projects, even though you have a contract. Too many times have I celebrated a million-dollar fee added to backlog, only to see it vanish after earning $25,000 on the feasibility phase. We can't set rules for what to include in backlog. There are guidelines, but they won't work without judgment.

32. Backlog per employee. This is an excellent indicator of future income. The only way to make money in this business is to have just a little more work to do than you have people to do it. If you are burning up backlog and hiring people, you will soon be losing money.

33. Backlog turnover. This ratio divides total active contracted backlog by average monthly billings. It tells you how many months of business you have in hand. It's a bit of an abstraction. Some contracts will extend for many months into the future. Even if no more work came in, the firm wouldn't stay at full force for those months and then dissolve all at once; projects would close one by one. Still, as the "burn rate" of your business, it is important to watch the trend.

34. Accounts receivable. This is the money your clients owe you. ARs are a chronic and intransigent irritant. Too many clients feel that the best way to raise cash is to delay paying their bills, and many professionals feel that it's unprofessional to dun their clients. That's wrong. It's bad business to let ARs go unattended.

ARs should be categorized as follows:

35. Current accounts receivable. This is the total money owed you, including the bills that just went out.

36. ARs over ninety days. This is the money that has been owed you for over ninety days. These accounts should get management attention and phone calls.

37. Accounts receivable turnover. This is the average collection period. It is calculated by dividing the total accounts receivable by the average billing per day. The average billing per day may be based on the average earned fee for the month or for the last quarter. A year is too much. If you have sixty-day turnover, it means that it is taking, on average, sixty days to get your clients to pay up.

*****

The P&L statement included here is a simple one appropriate for a small company or a consolidated report. As companies grow, most begin to subdivide the technical and administrative staff into groups. Line divisions that perform income-producing services can be treated as small companies—individual profit centers. Staff divisions such as accounting and marketing are cost centers.

When a project is handled by several profit centers, income must be divided among them. This means that you must measure the percent complete for the portion of the project that's being executed by each of the divisions. Each division will have overhead costs: time spent to manage the division, business development expenses, office supplies, secretarial labor, and so forth. To the extent that these costs can be controlled by the division manager, they should be assigned to the division.

Large brainpower firms typically have overhead-only departments in such areas as accounting, legal counsel, marketing, personnel, data processing, and office services. Costs incurred in these departments must be included in the financial reports reviewed by the people who manage those costs—the department managers. Corporate costs that aren't assignable to any division should be reviewed by the chief operating and executive officers of the firm.

*****

Numbers tell only part of the story. Levels of quality, innovation, and service are hard to summarize in financial reports. Many firms have failed because their managers concentrated only on financial reports while unnoticed time bombs of poor performance ticked away. Looking at the arithmetic of a profit and loss statement, it appears that one must simply reduce direct job costs and cut marketing and management costs to make money. Yet cutting the efforts that create these costs may destroy the company.

Conversely, managers who ignore the flow of time and money will get into trouble. Running a company requires knowing how much should be spent and when and where to chop. That's a tough job. It requires managers who have a clear view of the professional activities that create cost and the value of their results.